Dearly Departed

poems by

Hayley Bowen

Finishing Line Press
Georgetown, Kentucky

Dearly Departed

Copyright © 2022 by Hayley Bowen
ISBN 978-1-64662-825-4 First Edition
All rights reserved under International and Pan-American Copyright Conventions. No part of this book may be reproduced in any manner whatsoever without written permission from the publisher, except in the case of brief quotations embodied in critical articles and reviews.

ACKNOWLEDGMENTS

Portions for Foxes originally appeared in *Dunes Review*, Spring 2020.
Hummingbird originally appeared in *Pif*, Summer 2020.
Sonora originally appeared in *Three Peaks Review*, Spring 2018.

Publisher: Leah Huete de Maines
Editor: Christen Kincaid
Cover Art: Sara Potocsny
Author Photo: Luke Slate
Cover Design: Elizabeth Maines McCleavy

Order online: www.finishinglinepress.com
also available on amazon.com

Author inquiries and mail orders:
Finishing Line Press
PO Box 1626
Georgetown, Kentucky 40324
USA

Table of Contents

Petrichor 1

Requiem for a Ghost I 2

Desert Song 4

Joshua Tree 6

Forget-Me-Not 7

II 8

Migration 10

Palmistry 11

Proprioception 12

III 13

Tumbleweed 15

Love Letter to Orange 16

Notes on Falling 17

IV 18

Portions for Foxes 19

I Don't Believe in Unconditional Love 20

Swans 21

V 22

What I Learned from Orpheus and Lot 24

Hummingbird 25

Trees Never Really Heal 26

VI 27

Maps 28

January 10th 30

Requiem 32

Sonora 34

For Dr. Courtney Huse Wika, for giving me poetry.
For Thea, Clara, Makena, Johanna, Isabel, Matt, Katie,
my big brothers,
Mom and Dad—for always believing in me.
And for J. Thank you for all of it.
In memory of Gage McSpadden

Petrichor

I have been waiting
for centuries—
mouth open skyward
like a baby bird
toward a boastful sun.
And the old stone gods
rise from the sand,
surrounding me,
watching,
doubting.
But I stand,
steadfast sentry
in this desert,
always.

Requiem for a Ghost I

We had been driving for four or five hours when he exited the interstate and pulled into a small, unfamiliar town. We pulled into a gas station just off what appeared to be the main drag in town, filled the gas tank, stretched, peed. I texted my mom "somewhere in Wyoming" to let her know we were not dead in a ditch yet. Stephen and I carried on with our excited chatter about which brewery we'd visit once we reached Arizona, and how sunburned we were hoping to get in California as we pulled up to the run-down, wood paneled liquor store. It was presumably the only place open at 11:40 p.m. on a Thursday, and the fluorescent glow of the flat white lights bleached the oil-stained parking lot as we came to a halt. Stephen and I drank together pretty often. It was actually sort of the whole reason we met, and eventually how we became such close friends. So, walking into this liquor store felt compulsory enough. The girl behind the counter did not look old enough to be working in a liquor store, and barely looked up when we walked in. She glanced in our direction, popped her gum, and rolled her high blonde ponytail to the other side of her head and returned her attention to some apparently urgent messages on her cell phone.

Stephen seemed to be looking for something specific, and when I asked what he was after he told me, "There's this one IPA we drank here last time, we always used to get it together, I don't know if they have it though". I didn't know who the "we" was that he was referring to, and to be honest I barely registered the thought that he was referencing his connection to this town we were in. It's embarrassing to admit, but I assumed he meant an IPA that Stephen and I had often drank together, but I did not want to risk revealing that he remembered something about our times spent together that I didn't. I nodded, feigning understanding, and idled around, looking over the depressingly broad selection of cheap vodka. After opening and closing each glass cooler door three or four times, hoping to will the beer into existence, he came to settle on a six pack of Coors Banquet pounders. "Classic", I said with a laugh, and he smiled and said it was "our go-to." Here I paused a moment longer than I had before, this time knowing I was not included in this "our". At this point I felt like he assumed I knew what he meant, since I had attempted to lead him to believe such, and it felt too stupid to ask for clarification now. The girl behind the counter didn't even bother to ID us. She wordlessly ran his debit card and handed him the receipt to sign. Stephen attempted to crack a joke that she blatantly ignored, and I sharply exhaled through my nose, trying not to laugh at his pinched lips and wide eyes elicited by the unsuccessful landing of his pun.

Back in the car, we rolled down the deserted main street with neon signs sleepily winking at us from shop windows. As we crept along, Stephen told me the story of a long hard run that once brought him and the other half of the unknown us along this street, and up the unforgiving hill that we now climbed from the comfort and warmth of the car. Suddenly it was the image of this run, accompanied by someone native to this land, that brought me to the realization of why we pulled off into this seemingly insignificant southern Wyoming town. We were chasing as many ghosts as we were fleeing, but here the ghost was literal. This was not an unplanned pitstop; this was a pilgrimage.

Desert Song

It is too hot to sleep.
Our restless legs squirm in cots
in the screened-in porch,
baking beneath the residual heat
of the moon.

Beds and A/C are adult luxuries,
but what the grown-ups miss
in their red wine slumbers
are the whispers of bare feet
on dusty deck boards, our hands
praying to rusty springs, begging
the back door not to betray our secrets.

Gapped teeth and freckled foreheads flee
into the arms of the tamarisk groves,
licking the salt the weeping trees shed,
whisper-screaming our freedom cries
to the star-peppered sky above.

The daylight belongs to the river—
to the sunscreen oil slicks
casting rainbows onto green glass water,
to the Mexican beer we were too young
to drink but drank anyway,
to the sand that snuck its way
into the tinfoil wrapped sandwiches,
to the downriver wind tangling unbrushed hair.

But the night belongs to the desert,
to the mesa that crowns her,
to the wild things running barefoot
chasing burrows and ghosts,
to my brothers and the orange blazer
defying gravity on cliff faces,
to the wishes I forgot to make
on shooting stars.

Before dawn, we creep back
to our beds, forgetting about
the creak of the back door and our parents
will pretend not to wake, pretend
not to have noticed we had ever gone.

Joshua Tree

You pour sunshine down my throat
and I swallow.
The light lives here now—
in ribshade, in lampcage—
only escaping in bubbles
when your words turn my stomach inside out.

You're following me up,
climbing higher
and higher,
trying to touch the top
of the Joshua tree.

I don't want to be afraid
of the birds anymore,
of the echo of their windchime bones,
of their wing-born sandstorm
on the highway.

Your feet wobble on jagged jaws
and sandstone desert cliffs,
and I realize I've been scrambling
relentlessly up
with no concern for our route
back down.

I think the sunshine in me wants to go home.
That's why my face keeps searching for the sky
and finding yours.

Forget-Me-Not

Shards of periwinkle sky shudder
to the forest floor and are reborn.
Little buttons of blue with beating
yellow hearts bloom with
such fervent enthusiasm one might
think the world has turned
upside down. The sky has
interrupted the slick bed of mud
and pine needles that swallow
the sound of every footfall,
and we grow in waves,
so eager to share our petals,
waking up to kiss the bare soles
of passersby, not thinking to prickle
or cry when we are picked, plucked
from the soft earth that birthed us.
Tread lightly over these hallowed grounds—
my fragile friends are everywhere.
Look down, see how we stare back,
arms spread wide, begging to be
embraced, relocated, dying
to spread our sweet little smiles.
They say we are destructive,
devastating,
invasive,

but God,

aren't we beautiful?

II

Brandon died after he was struck by lightning, and he has been immortal ever since. I think the extremely bizarre situation that resulted in Brandon's death adds to the mystification of him. When I met Stephen, and the rest of our friends, Brandon had been gone for a year and six months, so the wound had healed enough for them to keep me distant from their grief—just distant enough for the story of Brandon to be told to me as fable. This man of the highest caliber, of purest heart, struck down by the unlikeliest of circumstances is the same man whose ghost I am now hunting in the dark of a forgotten town. I feel this same story-like disassociation with death very often. As if every person that I have known and lost is not really dead, or really gone, simply somewhere that is not here, existing now in the same realm that bedtime stories exist. Brandon is preserved there in that quiet plot in Wyoming's southern hills, but his ghost lives on everywhere his story still gets told. That's the thing that scares me most about ghosts—the possibility of never being one.

I don't think it's all that uncommon to fantasize about one's own death. And I don't mean fantasize in that I long for it the same way I fantasize about an IPA after work, or about a vacation in the sun, but rather fantasize in the sense that a morbid obsession is the result of my utter lack of control over the situation. When others die I feel the need to become closer to the dead, as if by proximity to their death I might begin to understand my own—and more importantly what becomes of me after I die. The only afterlife I believe in is the one that those I leave behind build for me, and the life I write down that will outlive me when I am gone.

In the most animalistic, reptile-brained way, we are programmed to fear death. Our reason for existence, in the basest most biological way, is to survive and reproduce, to ensure the continuation of our species. We have this in common with most species, but what makes us so distinctly human is fear of what comes next. Recall Hamlet: "But that dread of something after death,/The undiscovered country from whose bourne/No traveler returns ... /does make cowards of us all." What is left of us after we are gone? I don't fear a consciousness that will exist eternally, nor do I fear heaven or hell. I am afraid of ceasing to exist to those that outlive me. Our stories will live forever as long as people keep telling them, but have I done enough to be someone worth telling?

Migration

One day a butterfly will wake up in the light
with inherited memories of the three thousand miles
that put her there. She will not know the work or the wings
that preceded her but she will feel them, show their faces
in the black of her wings. Some day she will return home,
all that way back north, where the journey was started on her behalf,
where her map was made before she was herself, and she will drink
from the great grandchildren of the flowers that fed her mothers.
And she will be home again.

Palmistry

My Grammy places her hand over my own—
on the kitchen table in the trailer
where I learned to walk, to speak—
and I saw my own future.

Skin worn thin and delicate
like the membrane of an orange slice,
but peppered with evidence
of the recklessness of youth;
sun spotted and darkened
as an hours-ago peeled apple.
Raised like mountain ranges
are her carpals, crossed
by bulging blue rivers of veins.

We are organic things,
and like all things we rot.
In my family we do it with pleasure.
With pride.

Proprioception

I am still eleven,
still knock-kneed
and unafraid, still
stranded in the desert.

My only map home is this memory:

my mom on the sofa
through the window, reading
by pinstriped sunlight, giving
a eulogy for who I used to be, singing—

baby, you forgot to die young like you promised.

III

After a few more miles, we turned left off the street onto a neatly groomed gravel road, passing through the threshold of towering wrought iron gates, and the blanket of quiet that seems to cover all graveyards enveloped us. I turned the music way down until it was just a soft mumble, garbled by the gravel crunching beneath the tires. We were far enough from town here that the inky darkness of rural night was thick, barely diluted by the moon overhead. It took him a few laps through the cemetery to find the right row—it looked different in the dark, and it had been years—but he eventually found a familiar enough tree and we parked. He grabbed the beers, letting them dangle from his fingers at his side, looking like a man burdened with the weight of the world hanging from his left fingertips. Armed with only the feeble flashlights from our cellphones, we set off into the night, hunting his ghost. Meandering through the headstones and granite angels, I took notice of dates and names, always strangely struck in the deepest part of my gut when the gap between the years wasn't wide enough. We passed by two fresh mounds of dirt, side by side, with matching headstones. Stephen shuddered with a "yeesh," and I did not look hard enough to read the dates, afraid of the scary story my mind might tell me.

It didn't take us too long after passing the still-healing scars on the earth to find our man. His headstone was tall and wide, and the stone, peppered with quartz, glittered like frost in the blue-white lights projected by our phones. It was intricately engraved with the silhouette of a runner breaking through a pine-lined path. Below his name the inscription read: "You will find him on the trail." Suddenly, standing in the presence of this long overdue reunion, I became uncomfortably aware of the eyes of hundreds of forgotten lives, watching me watch them, using the voices of the wind in the grass and leaves to whisper *outsider*. And they were right; I did not belong there. I was intruding, unable to mourn a man I never knew. I hesitated in a purgatory of un-belonging. While I waited to be either saved or damned by Stephen's instruction, I mourned for him in place of the unfamiliar dead and let the grief of my uselessness play understudy to a loss I could never truly know. I wanted to run from Stephen and this unshakeable feeling of invading a private and sacred space, but I stayed, lost somewhere between supportive and intrusive. I knew I had no right to share in Brandon's story, I could only listen to it as his friends chose to tell it. But there in that graveyard, Stephen was writing another chapter for Brandon and for himself, and I was not meant to be involved in that plotline. I felt lifetimes pass, I felt the lifetimes cut short fill the air, causing the space and sky around us to inhale and exhale, until he at last seemed to remember I was present.

When he finally realized that the chattering was coming from my teeth in the cold of night and not the stirring of unsettled bones he said, "You don't have to stay if you want to go warm up in the car. I won't be long." It was so like him to find a polite way to tell me to go away, to leave him alone, to let him have this moment to himself. He gave me the illusion of a choice, but I recognized my cue at once. I took the car keys and turned on my heel to depart, but one of the restless spirits spun me back to face him. I pulled him to me and he pulled me back harder, silently saying—or I at least I hope he heard me—I love you's and I'm here for you's and I'm sorry's. As I turned away to take my leave and return to the world of the living, I saw him sink down to the grass, heard the *hiss—snap* of a beer can, and the catching up of two old friends commenced.

Tumbleweed

I feel like a tumbleweed
at the mercy of whatever I get lodged in:
no control over my body
or where I will end up.
Love, you are a semitruck that struck
me as I bounced down a forgotten desert highway
and now I am stuck.

Love, you are the driver
and the truck and I am powerless
and a pest, a weed for you
to weed out once you slow down
long enough to notice me
hitch-hiking in your grill and I'll
be discarded at some rest stop
along with the pop cans and candy wrappers
into a bin. Or maybe, if I'm lucky,

love, you'll set me free on the street
to wander the lonesome desert
following the river of cracked tar
until, invariably, you drive by
and hit me again.

Love Letter to Orange

Biting into the membrane of a clementine—
an eruption of sweet on my tongue—
you taste like 4pm in January,
when the light smooths out my roughest skin,
before the mountains bleed purple onto the horizon.

You smell like Coppertone and rust
and the tires of the Blazer kicking up dust on the mesa.
You smell like the salt of the weeping tamarisks,
and cattails blooming from the lagoon. You taste
like push pops from Mac's, sherbet running down my fist,
stickying my fingers in the too-fast-to-eat heat,
dyeing my wrist
with your kiss.

You taste like breakfast in bed,
like going to bed with a ghost, and
like sunglasses hung around his neck like a rosary.

You taste like sinking the boat and bailing
out the water with empty canisters of Sunny D,
and like card games and taking shots
out of antique teacups.

You taste like Cactus Cooler and vodka
in the moonlight, slipping in silt as I stumble
around the island's trail, alone this time, for the first time,
reaching for someone that isn't there.

Now, you taste like September.

Not the last time I saw him,
but the last time I believed he might love me.

Notes on Falling

You feel things the way a child does—
full fist into the boiling water,
no toe dipping or hesitation.
And you scream—
        oh god, you scream—
about how it burns,
how your flesh is bubbled
and boiled away.

And I don't know how to help you
besides saying

next time don't be so reckless.

Next time, don't dive in
without first checking the temperature
or peeking over the edge for rocks at the bottom
or finding out first
if there is a shark in the water.

So what I'm saying is
I don't know how to help you,
because I don't understand
what you're feeling; your nerves
singed down to the bone.

I have never treated love like anything
but a body of water
that could kill me,
and you have never stopped
seeming so eager to drown

IV

I can't help but wonder who would drink with me at my grave if I die young. What poem would be chosen to forever mark my body's final resting place? And even more than that, who would tell my story? I feel like I need to write anything down because at any given moment, I could be wiped out by a bus, or fall off of a cliff, or murdered by a jaded ex-lover, so I need to write everything down in case I become relevant after my death.

It is an odd sensation to desire to be known while being so insignificant in the grand scheme of things. Nobody has ever heard of me, or my writing, I do not have fans or a following, so why do I continue to document my days as if history has its eyes on me? And why do I feel like I need history to watch me? These questions are answerable by understanding my generation. The millennials exist as inbetweeners, with no great war and no revolution to define our place on the historical timeline. Since we won't be remembered as a side effect of the world we live in, we feel compelled to be remembered by what we create. The root of my compulsion to be remembered—and therefore to write—comes from the anxiety of living in a new kind of revolution. In my lifetime the world has seen the revolution of the internet and social media, and unless you happen to be one of the very few "social media famous" influencers, this generation will not be remembering your name. That is why I feel the need to do something truly spectacular, to one-up the instagrammers and youtubers of my time, and be special enough to be remembered. Brandon, in his kind and gentle ways, managed to be more than enough to be remembered, and his legacy will forever be echoed around the Black Hills of South Dakota.

Portions for Foxes

It is not in a vixen's nature
to abandon her young. Some ancient thing
decided long ago on her behalf
that she would be a mother.
But the instinct to survive is stronger.
So, when the rancher's wife found the fox,
her back leg a tangle of blood and barbed wire,
she let it go. She knew there must be pups nearby.
But with a ruined leg,
all twisted muscle and rust,
a fox cannot hunt enough
to feed herself and her pups,
she cannot spy, belly low, on the hens in the yard—
if she stays here she will starve.
She retreats to the tall grass
that laces the edge of the woods, leaving
her den behind her. If she stays
they will all starve.

They will not learn to leap and dive
like land-borne salmon through waves
of ambering grain—a gold lake
in the September sun.
They will not learn to hunt, to creep
quietly in the blind spots of rabbits,
and they will starve to death—
withdrawals from their mother's milk—
before their brand-new eyes even have time
to open.
The den will cave in with the snow
and their bodies will unite with the roots
of the brambles that grow
overhead, marking the graves then
spreading so wild you'd never know
the flesh below that feeds them.

I Don't Believe in Unconditional Love.

Who has a heart
with so many rooms
that can be filled with ghosts
haunting this house in my chest,
never to be exorcised?

I inhale sage
to clear you out,
to smudge away
a love I don't believe in,
no longer convinced
that the shadows are watching me back.
I have no ouija to invite you back in,
and I know now the creaking beams
are just echoes of my own blood
settling—not your footsteps still tapping
out a rhythm on the backside
of my sternum.

No I don't have room
for unconditional love.
Only two atriums
two ventricles
too small to let
a poltergeist stay.

Swans

I am suspicious of swans,
how they flaunt their long necks,
unafraid and exposed.
They drift like cottonwood seeds
across the July sky, unaware
or undisturbed by the way
their throats boast of vulnerability.

So catchable, so easy to strangle,
to tie in knots, to bite into
and tear apart, yet still, they drift,
slowly, eyes closed against the sun,
without urgency, resting their heads
on their chests. Maybe
what I mean to say is,
I am so envious of swans.

V

I'm not sure how much time passed, the two of us sitting alone in very different scenarios. Stephen returned with three crushed cans, the remaining two still dangling from their plastic noose. He apologized for taking so long, and I oversold my nonchalance and not-in-a-rush attitude. In truth I didn't mind how long the trip took, my only qualm was the time I did not get to spend beside him. The hyperawareness of our deteriorating timeline was never far from my mind.

Back in the densely wooded hills where this journey of ours began, our friends were preparing to run a race in the place that Brandon died. They run in his memory and honor every year, but this year Stephen and I fled westward. Brandon's friends, long since moved on, would return to those hills, to run and drink and laugh and commiserate, but Stephen would not be there to join them. I still feel guilty for keeping him away from this annual catharsis. That night in the graveyard, I wished more than anything that I was not too ignorant to know how to comfort him. Or maybe comfort for something like this doesn't exist. Maybe all I did was all I could have done. At least that's what I will choose to believe, too afraid to believe he could resent me for this time with him that I so treasured.

Naïvely, stupidly, I said, "It's almost better this way, isn't it? Getting to be here with him?" The Wyoming bluffs had begun to melt into swelling red rock and cliff faces as the night leaked by outside our windows. "No, it's not." He said it without any malice, no condescension or anger, only a wistful knowledge that I did not understand. "That was his body, but that's not him. You saw what was written on the stone? It's from a poem, I can show it to you sometime. It said *you will find him on the trail.* He'll be there, running with the guys this weekend".

I said nothing, watching the moonlight dance between the trees, reflected in his chocolate eyes. "When I'm out there, hurting in the canyon on a hard run, I can still hear him. Bullshitting, laughing at me," he laughed a little, certainly recalling a specific session of suffering. "He's out there, in the hills." There is the truth behind all ghost stories: someone is only ever truly gone once their story stops being told. Brandon will live forever, running through Spearfish Canyon, through the rolling Wyoming hills, the places that his story gets passed down.

I realized that I was jealous of Brandon on some level. He and Stephen shared something I will never understand. Part of that is that I never knew Brandon. Part of that is that I am still alive, and he is not. But I was jealous also for a future that hasn't happened yet. I was jealous because I felt that I have not been kind or gentle or substantial enough to warrant midnight visits and beers at my grave. That if I were to die tragically, Stephen—and the rest of my friends and peers—would only remember me as an acquaintance. I understand how sick it is to envy the dead, to envy someone who had no say in his death and who people miss and ache for daily, but as ugly as it might be, I was jealous. So, the preservation of myself in writing has become almost a compulsion. I channel this morbid and grotesque jealousy into creative productivity. I record everything meticulously, terrified of forgetting or being forgotten. I write as if by writing it down, it will all become immortal.

What I Learned from Orpheus and Lot

I remember last December the way
I remember a fever— in dizzy half-dreams
and shivers and sweats. Sometimes I wonder
if my heat-oppressèd brain imagined it all:

the snow falling like bitter tears as we sat
on the curb outside the False Bottom bar,
the way I swore you'd never see me again,
your white-hot denial,
the way I was right.

Or the way, as I walked away,
I swear I heard you calling my name.
Or the vertigo of half-knowing
some half-forgotten fairytale,

that as soon as I turned around
the fever would break
and the cold bite of the night would sink in
and I'd be left with nothing but a mound of salt

and memory.

Hummingbird

Most days I try to forget you ever existed,
but I comfort myself by reciting,
it's because you were never meant to.
You were the worst kind of miracle,
a fraction of a fraction of an odd, sad anomaly.
It's not your fault. You were never viable.

One year ago, you were the size of a hummingbird's egg,
hidden away in the dark, almost undetectable,
but your hatching was interrupted, and you were lost.
Looking back, I think I knew somewhere deep down
that you had made a nest of me, but it was easier
to believe you were something more mundane.

Somedays I feel caged by the weight of not being able to save you,
as if my wings were clipped in punishment
because you never had the chance to see the sky.
Somedays I feel the wingbeats of hummingbirds
battering my heart until it buckles.
Somedays are nothing but an unbearably empty perch.

Trees never really heal

from sun-scalding and scarring.
they simply cover up the wound
with new bark. But peel it back—
layers of rough shell—and see
the marred pulp, interrupting the rings
like smeared ink on a map; an attempt
to erase a history that is still
so raw, so present, and visible
just beneath the surface.
Trees never really heal, only learn

to hide,
and keep growing.

VI

Over the stereo, Shakey Graves crooned out, *you and I both know that the house is haunted, and you and I both know that the ghost is me.* We sang along, trying to imitate the singer's soulful rasp. It became one of "our" songs, and all our ghosts from that trip still seep out every time I hear it. Stephen pressed down on the gas pedal, accelerating toward the next chapter, toward the stories that we set out to write in the Californian desert. We let the secrets of that place be kept by ink and the moonlight, leaving both of our ghosts in the review mirror, fading with the dark highway behind us.

Maps

Turn left onto I-90 West
for fifty miles of small talk and soft plans.

Turn left for WY-50 South
for fifty miles of impromptu talk therapy.

Turn right for WY-387 West
for thirty-two miles of songs we used to dance to
on the sticky wood floor of your old place,
soaked in sweat and cheap beer.

Merge onto I-25 South
for twenty miles of memories of when
it was warmer, when all of this was lighter—
hot skies and cold creeks and smoky nights.

Merge onto I-80 West.
Now entering Utah.
Jokes about getting kicked out—banned for life—
over our shared affinity
for coffee and beer and pre-marital sex.

Continue for two hundred and sixty miles
of ghost stories, but not the ghosts from the attic
or that '40's film that you love because I love,
but the ghosts of flesh and blood that occupy
those black hills we flee from.

Sunrise in Moab.
Gas station breakfast burritos
and cell phone photoshoots
and not nearly enough coffee.

A changing of the guard.
You sleep
through Nevada and Arizona,
but not soundly.

Keep left at fork, follow signs for Phoenix.
Three hundred and eighty-one miles of podcasts
and the poor unfortunate souls who met
an untimely demise on their way to California.
Pioneer prophecies.

Merge onto US-95 South.
Now entering California.
Pull over here, take a picture with the sign,
arms wrapped around each other's road-worn bodies.

You have arrived.

And there in the heat,
in the cracking leather seats of the Blazer,
and in the bath-warm river,
and at the kitchen table, playing card games,
I fell in love while we fell apart.

Everything moves slower in places like this,
keeping pace with the laze of the lagoon out back.

Your honey eyes in emerald water,
Mexican beer and damp bedsheets.

One thousand, two hundred, and fifty-one miles
until we get back home,
haunted by sunburn and secrets and memory.

January 10th, after a pleasant nightmare

The lagoon is shattered by white light,
like so many diamonds, blinding,
beckoning to be mined from the green water.

The fat grey geese break the current
like boulders in a stream,
coal-black eyes twinkling, reflecting
either the water's sparkle or their own hope
for croutons from my sundried hands.

At night the water turns to glass,
and the moon hasn't been so full
since you were here with me, sweating
on top of the sheets in midnight heat,
your tongue some poison potion
of Pacifico and *we can't*.

It's been sixteen months since we left
this place together, and six weeks
since we said goodbye. Why
are you still here?

When I see the geese swimming,
I see you swimming after them.
When I smell the silt and hot dirt
I smell your breath, your hair gel,
your sweat.

I couldn't sleep in the bedroom we once shared,
but then I could not sleep at all
so I compromised. I brought the mattress
that still cradles the impression of your ghost
into a different room, and in the dark

I almost feel the weight of you next to me.
Not touching me.

Not allowed to.
Straining to recall a time
when I believed we could
be.

Requiem

The brights on my car are no match
for the inky blackness of the desert.
The road ahead of me reflects the winks of mile markers
and tumbleweeds, but beyond the road I am adrift
in a sea of night. I know the curtain of shadow
conceals sleeping giants: saguaros and mesas
and the crag of Palo Verde peak—the jewel
of a mountain range that encases the town
in a crown of rugged crests. Here—
in this town with one road, one stop sign, no streetlights—
you will be waiting for me. I will find you
on the white plank bridge, where the death rattles
of summer coerce the cattails to dance in shivering water,
the lagoon erupting into glistening emeralds. I will find you
descending down-stream, guided by the blazing moon,
in the midnight heat that glares unconcerned
with the absence of the sun. I will find you in curio shops
whose formerly photo-perfect windows now bear
the burden of boards and nails, and in bonfire barrels
and Pacifico bottles. You will be there in the hands
of my childhood, the ones I used to clasp in prayer, begging
the rusty springs of the back door not to betray
the secrets of my late-night escapades, and
in the secrets you kept—pretending not to have woken
at the creak of those dusty deck boards, and you will be there
in the garage with the boat that never ran right,
and dozing in an arm chair, red-wine sunset slumber,
and stationed at the grill, the steadfast sentry
of our every evening supper. I will find you in the miles
of unmapped canyon lands, in the salty embrace
of the tamarisk groves, in the cactus-strewn washes,
chasing burrows and ghosts. I will find you in sandstone
caves dripping in amethyst and obsidian,
in the gunpowder sky's violet bruises that still bloom
on the ocotillo horizon, in the blizzards of biting earth

that still blossom from the ground up. You will be there
in the requiem the river sings for you,
the Canyon of the Gargoyles humming the harmony,
and I will find you in the stone-sided house—
that all but forgotten oasis—
waiting.

Sonora

There are no blizzard forecasts
in the place it does not snow.
In my mind it is always warm here,
but the sun shines cold and bleak,
and Tasmanian devil clouds blossom
from the ground up—
whipping winds of crushed glass and bones;
a blizzard of biting earth.
What's the opposite of snowfall?

Sandrise?

It's a supernova of suffocation,
and what remains is a gunpowder sky:
violet bruises blooming on a clementine horizon,
and hair and lips and skin covered in
sand and sweat and secrets.
No avalanche, no downed powerlines, no felled trees.
It is gone as quickly as it came.
The only evidence of the violence
are sand-scratched eyelids.
This desert's only permanence is that
in this place it does not snow.

www.ingramcontent.com/pod-product-compliance
Lightning Source LLC
LaVergne TN
LVHW040116080426
835507LV00041B/1062